CU00677492

Praying the Psalms

by
Pope Benedict XVI

*All booklets are published thanks to the
generous support of the members of the
Catholic Truth Society*

CATHOLIC TRUTH SOCIETY
PUBLISHERS TO THE HOLY SEE

Contents

ISBN 978 1 86082 855 3

"Arise, O Lord! Deliver me!"

Psalm 3: King David needs help

Today we are resuming the Audiences in St Peter's Square and the "school of prayer" which we attend together during these Wednesday Catecheses. I would like to begin by meditating on several Psalms, which, as I said last June, constitute the "prayer book" par excellence. The first Psalm I shall consider is a Psalm of lamentation and supplication, imbued with deep trust, in which the certainty of God's presence forms the basis of the prayer that springs from the condition of extreme peril in which the person praying finds himself. It is Psalm 3, which Jewish tradition ascribes to David at the moment when he fled from his son Absalom (cf. v. 1): this was one of the most dramatic and anguishing episodes in the king's life, when his son usurped his royal throne and forced him to flee from Jerusalem for his life (cf. *2 S* 15ff). Thus David's plight and anxiety serve as a background to this prayer and help us to understand it by representing a typical situation in which such a Psalm may be recited. Every man and woman can recognise in the Psalmist's cry those feelings of sorrow, bitter regret and yet at the same time trust in God, who, as the Bible tells us, had accompanied David on the flight from his city.

An urgent plea

The Psalm opens with an invocation to the Lord:

"O Lord, how many are my foes!
Many are rising against me;
many are saying of me,
'There is no help for him in God'" (vv. 2-3).

The praying man's description of the situation is therefore marked by intensely dramatic tones. The idea of "multitude" is conveyed with the triple use of "many" - three words that in the original text are different terms with the same Hebrew root so as to give further emphasis to the enormity of the danger - in a repetitive manner, as it were, hammering it in. This insistence on the large number of his enemies serves to express the Psalmist's perception of the absolute disproportion between him and his persecutors, which justifies and establishes the urgency of his plea for help; his oppressors are numerous, they get the upper hand, whereas the man praying is alone and defenceless, at the mercy of his assailants. Yet the first word the Psalmist says is "Lord"; his cry opens with a call to God. A multitude threatens him and rises against him, generating fear that magnifies the threat, making it appear greater and even more terrifying; but the praying person does not let this vision of death prevail, he keeps intact his relationship with the God of life and turns to him first in search of help.

Spiritual temptation

However, his enemies attempt to break this bond with God and to injure their victim's faith. They insinuate that the Lord cannot intervene, they say that not even God can save him. Hence the attack is not only physical but involves the spiritual dimension too: "there is no help for him in God", they say, targeting the central principle of the Psalmist's mind. This is the extreme temptation to which the believer is subjected, the temptation to lose faith, to lose trust in God's closeness. The righteous pass the final test, remain steadfast in faith, in the certainty of the truth and in full trust in God; in this way they find life and truth. It seems to me that here the Psalm touches us very personally: beset by many problems we are tempted to think that perhaps God will not save me, that he does not know me, perhaps he is not able to; the temptation to lose faith is our enemy's ultimate attack and if we are to find God, if we are to find life, we must resist it.

The Lord responds and saves

Thus in our Psalm the person praying is called to respond with faith to the attacks of the wicked: his foes - as I said - deny that God can help him; yet he invokes God, he calls him by name, "Lord", and then turns to him with an emphatic "thou/you" that expresses a solid, sturdy relationship and implies the certainty of the divine response:

"But you, O Lord are a shield about me,
my glory, and the lifter of my head.
I cry aloud to the Lord,
and he answers me from his holy hill" (vv. 4-5).

The vision of the enemies then disappears; they have not triumphed because the one who believes in God is sure that God is his friend. Only the "thou/you" of God is left. Now only One opposes the "many", but this One is far greater, far more powerful, than many adversaries. The Lord is help, defence and salvation; as a shield he protects the person who entrusts himself to him and enables him to lift his head in the gesture of triumph and victory. Man is no longer alone, his foes are not invincible as they had seemed, for the Lord hears the cry of the oppressed and answers from the place of his presence, from his holy hill.

God protects those who believe in him

The human being cries out in anguish, in danger, in pain; the human being calls for help and God answers. In this interweaving of the human cry and the divine response we find the dialectic of prayer and the key to reading the entire history of salvation. The cry expresses the need for help and appeals to the other's faithfulness; crying out means making an act of faith in God's closeness and in his willingness to listen. Prayer expresses the certainty of a divine presence already experienced and believed in, which is fully expressed in God's salvific answers. This is important: that in our prayer the certainty of God's presence be given importance and be made present. Thus the Psalmist, who feels besieged by death, professes his faith in the God of life who, as a shield, surrounds him with an invulnerable protection; the one who believed he was as good as lost can raise his head because the Lord saves him; the praying person, threatened and mocked, is in glory, because God is his glory.

God's presence is reassuring

The divine response that hears his prayer totally reassures the Psalmist; even his fear is no more and his cry is soothed in peace, in deep inner tranquillity.

> "I lie down and sleep; I wake again,
> for the Lord sustains me.
> I am not afraid of ten thousands of people
> who have set themselves against me round about" (vv. 6-7).

The praying person, even in peril, in the midst of battle, can sleep serenely in an unequivocal attitude of trusting abandonment. His foes have pitched camp around him, they are numerous, they besiege him, they rise up against him, taunting and trying to make him fall; instead he lies down and sleeps, calm and serene, sure of God's presence. And, on reawakening he finds God still beside him, as a custodian who does not fall asleep (cf. *Ps* 121[120]:3-4), who sustains him, who holds his hand, who never abandons him. The fear of death is vanquished by the presence of One who never dies. And even the night that is peopled by atavistic fears, the sorrowful night of solitude and anguished waiting is now transformed: what evoked death became the presence of the Eternal One.

Divine liberation

The enemy's visible, massive, impressive attack is countered by the invisible presence of God with all his invincible power. And it is to him that the Psalmist, after his trusting words, once again addresses the prayer: "Arise, O Lord! Deliver me, O my God!" (v. 8a). His assailants "are rising" (cf. v. 2) against their victim; instead the One who will "arise" is the Lord and it will be to defeat them. God will deliver him, answering his cry. Thus the Psalm ends with the vision of liberation from the peril that kills, and from the temptation that can cause us to perish. After addressing his plea to the Lord to arise and deliver him, the praying person describes the divine victory: the enemies - who with their unjust and cruel oppression are the symbol of all that opposes God and his plan of salvation - are defeated. Struck on the mouth, they will no longer attack with their destructive violence and will be unable to instil evil and doubt in God's presence and action. Their senseless and blasphemous talk is denied once and for all and is reduced to silence by the Lord's saving intervention (cf. v. 8bc). In this way the Psalmist can conclude his prayer with a sentence with liturgical connotations that celebrates the God of life in gratitude and praise: "Deliverance belongs to the Lord; your blessing be upon your people" (v. 9).

The certainty of faith

Psalm 3 has presented us with a supplication full of trust and consolation. In praying this Psalm, we can make our own the sentiments of the Psalmist, a figure of the righteous person persecuted, who finds his fulfilment in Jesus. In sorrow, in danger, in the bitterness of misunderstanding and offence the words of the Psalm open our hearts to the comforting certainty of faith. God is always close - even in difficulties, in problems, in the darkness of life - he listens and saves in his own way. However, it is necessary to recognise his presence and accept his ways, as did David in his humiliating flight from his son, Absalom; as did the just man who is persecuted in the Book of Wisdom and, ultimately and completely, as did the Lord Jesus on Golgotha. And when, in the eyes of the wicked, God does not seem to intervene and the Son dies, it is then that the true glory and the definitive realisation of salvation is manifest to all believers. May the Lord give us faith, may he come to our aid in our weakness and make us capable of believing and praying in every anxiety, in the sorrowful nights of doubt and the long days of sorrow, abandoning ourselves with trust to him, who is our "shield" and our "glory".

"My God, my God, why have you forsaken me?"

Psalm 22 (21): A prayer of supplication

In the Catechesis today I would like to look at a Psalm with strong Christological implications which continually surfaces in accounts of Jesus' passion, with its twofold dimension of humiliation and glory, of death and life. It is Psalm 22 according to the Hebrew tradition and Psalm 21 according to the Graeco-Latin tradition, a heartfelt, moving prayer with a human density and theological richness that make it one of the most frequently prayed and studied Psalms in the entire Psalter. It is a long poetic composition and we shall reflect in particular on its first part, centred on the lament, in order to examine in depth certain important dimensions of the prayer of supplication to God.

This Psalm presents the figure of an innocent man, persecuted and surrounded by adversaries who clamour for his death; and he turns to God with a sorrowful lament which, in the certainty of his faith, opens mysteriously to praise. The anguishing reality of the present and the consoling memory of the past alternate in his prayer in an agonised awareness of his own desperate situation in which, however, he does not want to give up hope. His initial cry is an appeal addressed to a God who appears remote, who does not answer and seems to have abandoned him:

"My God, my God, why have you forsaken me?
Why are you so far from helping me,
from the words of my groaning?
O my God, I cry by day, but you do not answer;
and by night, but find no rest" (vv. 3-4).

The Psalmist's faith remains strong

God is silent and this silence pierces the soul of the person praying, who ceaselessly calls but receives no answer. Day and night succeed one another in an unflagging quest for a word, for help that does not come; God seems so distant, so forgetful, so absent. The prayer asks to be heard, to be answered, it begs for contact, seeks a relationship that can give comfort and salvation. But if God fails to respond, the cry for help is lost in the void and loneliness becomes unbearable. Yet, in his cry, the praying man of our Psalm calls the Lord "my" God at least three times, in an extreme act of trust and faith. In spite of all appearances, the Psalmist cannot believe that his link with the Lord is totally broken and while he asks the reason for a presumed incomprehensible abandonment, he says that "his" God cannot forsake him.

The Psalm in Jesus Christ

As is well known, the initial cry of the Psalm, "My God, my God, why have you forsaken me?", is recorded by the Gospels of Matthew and Mark as the cry uttered by Jesus dying on the Cross (cf. *Mt* 27:46, *Mk* 15:34). It expresses all the desolation of the Messiah, Son of God, who is facing the drama of death, a reality totally opposed to the Lord of life. Forsaken by almost all his followers, betrayed and denied by the disciples, surrounded by people who insult him, Jesus is under the crushing weight of a mission that was to pass through humiliation and annihilation. This is why he cried out to the Father, and his suffering took up the sorrowful words of the Psalm. But his is not a desperate cry, nor was that of the Psalmist who, in his supplication, takes a tormented path which nevertheless opens out at last into a perspective of praise, into trust in the divine victory. And since in the Jewish custom citing the beginning of a Psalm implied a reference to the whole poem, although Jesus' anguished prayer retains its burden of unspeakable suffering, it unfolds to the certainty of glory. "Was it not necessary that the Christ should suffer these things and enter into his glory?", the Risen Christ was to say to the disciples at Emmaus (*Lk* 24:26). In his passion, in obedience to the Father, the Lord Jesus passes through abandonment and death to reach life and to give it to all believers.

A history of faith

This initial cry of supplication in our Psalm 22[21] is followed in sorrowful contrast by the memory of the past,

"In you our fathers trusted;
they trusted, and you did deliver them.
To you they cried, and were saved;
in you they trusted, and were not disappointed" (vv. 5-6).

The God who appears today to be so remote to the Psalmist, is nonetheless the merciful Lord whom Israel experienced throughout its history. The people to whom the praying person belongs are the object of God's love, and can witness to his fidelity to him. Starting with the Patriarchs, then in Egypt and on the long pilgrimage through the wilderness, in the stay in the promised land in contact with aggressive and hostile peoples, to the night of the exile, the whole of biblical history is a history of a cry for help on the part of the People and of saving answers on the part of God. And the Psalmist refers to the steadfast faith of his ancestors who "trusted" - this word is repeated three times - without ever being disappointed. Then, however, it seems that this chain of trusting invocations and divine answers has been broken; the Psalmist's situation seems to deny the entire history of salvation, making the present reality even more painful.

The Psalmist prays for pity

God, however, cannot deny him help; so here the prayer returns to describing the distressing plight of the praying person, as he induces the Lord to have pity on him and to intervene, as he always had done in the past. The Psalmist describes himself as "a worm, and no man, scorned by men, and despised by the people" (v. 7). He was mocked, people made grimaces at him, (cf. v. 8), and his faith was wounded. "He committed his cause to the Lord; let him deliver him, let him rescue him, for he delights in him!" (v. 9), they said. Under the jeering blows of irony and contempt, it almost seems as though the persecuted man loses his own human features, like the suffering servant outlined in the Book of Isaiah (cf. 52:14; 53:2b-3). And like the oppressed righteous man in the Book of Wisdom (cf. 2:12-20), like Jesus on Calvary (cf. *Mt* 27:39-43), the Psalmist saw his own relationship with the Lord called into question in the cruel and sarcastic emphasis of what is causing him to suffer: God's silence, his apparent absence.

God has always been present

And yet God was present with an indisputable tenderness in the life of the person praying. The Psalmist reminds the Lord of this: "Yet you are he who took me from the womb; you did keep me safe upon my mother's breasts. Upon you was I cast from my birth" (vv. 10-11a). The Lord is the God of life who brings the newborn child into the world and cares for him with a father's affection. And though the memory of God's fidelity in the history of the people has first been recalled, the praying person now re-evokes his own personal history of relations with the Lord, going back to the particularly significant moment of the beginning of his life. And here, despite the desolation of the present, the Psalmist recognises a closeness and a divine love so radical that he can now exclaim, in a confession full of faith and generating hope: "and since my mother bore me you have been my God" (v. 11b).

Fear and violence

The lament then becomes a heartfelt plea: "Be not far from me, for trouble is near and there is none to help" (v. 12). The only closeness that the Psalmist could perceive and that filled him with fear was that of his enemies. It was therefore necessary for God to make himself close and to help him, because enemies surrounded the praying man, they encircled him and were like strong bulls, like ravening and roaring lions (cf. vv. 13-14). Anguish alters his perception of the danger, magnifying it. The adversaries seem invincible, they become ferocious, dangerous animals, while the Psalmist is like a small worm, powerless and defenceless. Yet these images used in the Psalm also serve to describe that when man becomes brutal and attacks his brother, something brutal within him takes the upper hand, he seems to lose any human likeness; violence always has something bestial about it and only God's saving intervention can restore humanity to human beings. Now, it seems to the Psalmist, the object of so much ferocious aggression, that he no longer has any way out and death begins to take possession of him: "I am poured out like water, and all my bones are out of joint… my strength is dried up like a potsherd, and my tongue cleaves to my jaws… they divide my garments among them, and for my raiment they cast lots" (vv.15,16,19). The disintegration of the body of the condemned man is described with the dramatic images that we encounter in the accounts of Christ's passion, the unbearable parching thirst that torments the dying man that is echoed in Jesus' request "I thirst" (cf. *Jn* 19:28), until we reach the definitive act of his tormentors, who, like the soldiers at the foot of the cross divide the clothes of the victim whom they consider already dead (cf. *Mt* 27:35; *Mk* 15:24; *Lk* 23:34; *Jn* 19:23-24).

Supplication becomes praise

Here then, impelling, once again comes the request for help: "But you, O Lord, be not far off! O you my help, hasten to my aid!... Save me" (vv. 20; 22a). This is a cry that opens the Heavens, because it proclaims a faith, a certainty that goes beyond all doubt, all darkness and all desolation. And the lament is transformed, it gives way to praise in the acceptance of salvation: "He has heard… I will tell of your name to my brethren; in the midst of the congregation I will praise you" (vv. 22c-23). In this way the Psalm opens to thanksgiving, to the great final hymn that sweeps up the whole people, the Lord's faithful, the liturgical assembly, the generations to come (cf. vv. 24-32). The Lord went to the rescue, he saved the poor man and showed his merciful face. Death and life are interwoven in an inseparable mystery and life triumphs, the God of salvation shows himself to be the undisputed Lord whom all the ends of the earth will praise and before whom all the families of the nations will bow down. It is the victory of faith which can transform death into the gift of life, the abyss of sorrow into a source of hope.

Humiliation leads to exaltation

This Psalm has taken us to Golgotha, to the foot of the cross of Jesus, to relive his passion and to share the fruitful joy of the resurrection. Let us therefore allow ourselves to be invaded by the light of the paschal mystery even in God's apparent absence, even in God's silence, and, like the disciples of Emmaus, let us learn to discern the true reality beyond appearances, recognising humiliation itself as the way to exaltation, and the cross as the full manifestation of life in death. Thus, replacing in God the Father all our trust and hope, in every anxiety we will be able to pray to him with faith, and our cry of help will be transformed into a hymn of praise.

"The Lord is my shepherd: I shall not want"

Psalm 23

Turning to the Lord in prayer implies a radical act of trust, in the awareness that one is entrusting oneself to God who is good, "merciful and gracious, slow to anger, and abounding in steadfast love and faithfulness" (*Ex* 34:6-7; *Ps* 86[85]:15; cf. *Jl* 2:13; *Jon* 4:2; *Ps* 103 [102]:8; 145[144]:8; *Ne* 9:17). For this reason I would like to reflect with you today on a Psalm that is totally imbued with trust, in which the Psalmist expresses his serene certainty that he is guided and protected, safe from every danger, because the Lord is his Shepherd. It is Psalm 23 [22, according to the Graeco-Latin numbering], a text familiar to all and loved by all.

The Lord is my shepherd

"The Lord is my shepherd, I shall not want": the beautiful prayer begins with these words, evoking the nomadic environment of sheep-farming and the experience of familiarity between the shepherd and the sheep that make up his little flock. The image calls to mind an atmosphere of trust, intimacy and tenderness: the shepherd knows each one of his sheep and calls them by name; and they follow him because they recognise him and trust in him (cf. *Jn*

10:2-4). He tends them, looks after them as precious possessions, ready to defend them, to guarantee their well-being and enable them to live a peaceful life. They can lack nothing as long as the shepherd is with them. The Psalmist refers to this experience by calling God his shepherd and letting God lead him to safe pastures:

"He makes me lie down in green pastures.
He leads me beside still waters;
he restores my soul.
He leads me in paths of righteousness
for his name's sake" (*Ps* 23[22]:2-3).

Grass and fresh water

The vision that unfolds before our eyes is that of green pastures and springs of clear water, oases of peace to which the shepherd leads his flock, symbols of the places of life towards which the Lord leads the Psalmist, who feels like the sheep lying on the grass beside a stream, resting rather than in a state of tension or alarm, peaceful and trusting, because it is a safe place, the water is fresh and the shepherd is watching over them. And let us not forget here that the scene elicited by the Psalm is set in a land that is largely desert, on which the scorching sun beats down, where the Middle-Eastern semi-nomad shepherd lives with his flock in the parched steppes that surround the villages. Nevertheless the shepherd knows where to find grass and fresh water, essential to life, he can lead the way to oases in which the soul is "restored" and where it is possible to recover strength and new energy to start out afresh on the journey.

As the Psalmist says, God guides him to "green pastures" and "still waters", where everything is superabundant, everything is given in plenty. If the Lord is the Shepherd, even in the desert, a desolate place of death, the certainty of a radical presence of life is not absent, so that he is able to say "I shall not want". Indeed, the shepherd has at heart the good of his flock, he adapts his own pace and needs to those of his sheep, he walks and lives with them, leading them on paths "of righteousness", that is, suitable for them, paying attention to their needs and not to his own. The safety of his sheep is a priority for him and he complies with this in leading his flock.

In God we find comfort

If we follow the "Good Shepherd" - no matter how difficult, tortuous or long the pathways of our life may seem, even through spiritual deserts without water and under the scorching sun of rationalism - with the guidance of Christ the Good Shepherd, we too, like the Psalmist, may be sure that we are walking on "paths of righteousness" and that the Lord is leading us, is ever close to us, and that we "shall lack nothing". For this reason the Psalmist can declare his calm assurance without doubt or fear:

"Even though I walk through the valley of the shadow
of death,
I fear no evil; for you are with me;
your rod and your staff
they comfort me" (v. 4).

Those who walk with the Lord even in the dark valleys
of suffering, doubt and all the human problems, feel safe.
You are with me: this is our certainty, this is what supports
us. The darkness of the night frightens us with its shifting
shadows, with the difficulty of distinguishing dangers, with
its silence taut with strange sounds. If the flock moves after
sunset when visibility fades, it is normal for the sheep to be
restless, there is the risk of stumbling or even of straying
and getting lost, and there is also the fear of possible
assailants lurking in the darkness. To speak of the "dark"
valley, the Psalmist uses a Hebrew phrase that calls to mind
the shadows of death, which is why the valley to be passed
through is a place of anguish, terrible threats, the danger of
death. Yet the person praying walks on in safety, undaunted
since he knows that the Lord is with him. "You are with
me" is a proclamation of steadfast faith and sums up the
radical experience of faith; God's closeness transforms
the reality, the dark valley loses all danger, it is emptied
of every threat. Now the flock can walk in tranquillity,
accompanied by the familiar rhythmical beat of the staff
on the ground, marking the shepherd's reassuring presence.

The Lord is the perfect host

This comforting image ends the first part of the Psalm, and gives way to a different scene. We are still in the desert, where the shepherd lives with his flock, but we are now set before his tent which opens to offer us hospitality.

"You prepare a table before me
in the presence of my enemies;
you anoint my head with oil,
my cup overflows" (v. 5).

The Lord is now presented as the One who welcomes the person praying with signs of generous hospitality, full of attention. The divine host lays the food on the "table", a term which in Hebrew means, in its primitive sense, the animal skin that was spread out on the ground and on which the food for the common meal was set out. It is a gesture of sharing, not only of food but also of life in an offering of communion and friendship that creates bonds and expresses solidarity. Then there is the munificent gift of scented oil poured on the head, which with its fragrance brings relief from the scorching of the desert sun, refreshes and calms the skin and gladdens the spirit. Lastly, the cup overflowing with its exquisite wine, shared with superabundant generosity, adds a note of festivity. Food, oil and wine are gifts that bring life and give joy, because they go beyond what is strictly necessary and express the free giving and abundance of love. Psalm

104[103] proclaims: "You cause the grass to grow for the cattle, and plants for man to cultivate, that he may bring forth food from the earth, and wine to gladden the heart of man, oil to make his face shine, and bread to strengthen man's heart" (vv. 14-15). The Psalmist becomes the object of much attention for which reason he sees himself as a wayfarer who finds shelter in a hospitable tent, whereas his enemies have to stop and watch, unable to intervene, since the one whom they considered their prey has been led to safety and has become a sacred guest who cannot be touched. And the Psalmist is us, if we truly are believers in communion with Christ. When God opens his tent to us to receive us, nothing can harm us.

Journey becomes pilgrimage

Then when the traveller sets out afresh, the divine protection is extended and accompanies him on his journey:

"Surely, goodness and mercy shall follow me
all the days of my life;
and I shall dwell in the house of the Lord
for ever" (*Ps* 23[22]:6).

The goodness and faithfulness of God continue to escort the Psalmist who comes out of the tent and resumes his journey. But it is a journey that acquires new meaning and becomes a pilgrimage to the Temple of the Lord, the holy place in which the praying person wants to "dwell" for ever and to which he also wants to "return". The Hebrew verb used here has the meaning of "to return" but with a small vowel change can be understood as "to dwell". Moreover, this is how it is rendered by the ancient versions and by the majority of the modern translations. Both meanings may be retained: to return and dwell in the Temple as every Israelite desires, and to dwell near God, close to him and to goodness. This is what every believer yearns and longs for: truly to be able to live where God is, close to him. Following the Shepherd leads to God's house, this is the destination of every journey, the longed for oasis in the desert, the tent of shelter in escaping from enemies, a place of peace where God's kindness and faithful love may be felt, day after day, in the serene joy of time without end.

Psalm 23 fulfilled in the Bible

With their richness and depth the images of this Psalm have accompanied the whole of the history and religious experience of the People of Israel and also accompany Christians. The figure of the shepherd, in particular, calls to mind the original time of the Exodus, the long journey through the desert, as a flock under the guidance of the divine Shepherd (cf. *Is* 63:11-14; *Ps* 77:20-21; 78:52-54). And in the Promised Land, the king had the task of tending the Lord's flock, like David, the shepherd chosen by God and a figure of the Messiah (cf. *2 S* 5:1-2; 7:8 *Ps*

78[77]:70-72). Then after the Babylonian Exile, as it were in a new Exodus (cf. *Is* 40:3-5,9-11; 43:16-21), Israel was brought back to its homeland like a lost sheep found and led by God to luxuriant pastures and resting places (cf. *Ezk* 34:11-16,23-31). However, it is in the Lord Jesus that all the evocative power of our Psalm reaches completeness, finds the fullness of its meaning: Jesus is the "Good Shepherd" who goes in search of lost sheep, who knows his sheep and lays down his life for them (cf. *Mt* 18:12-14; *Lk* 15:4-7; *Jn* 10:2-4,11-18). He is the way, the right path that leads us to life (cf. *Jn* 14:6), the light that illuminates the dark valley and overcomes all our fears (cf. *Jn* 1:9; 8:12; 9:5; 12:46). He is the generous host who welcomes us and rescues us from our enemies, preparing for us the table of his body and his blood (cf. *Mt* 26:26-29; *Mk* 14:22-25); *Lk* 22:19-20) and the definitive table of the messianic banquet in heaven (cf. *Lk* 14:15ff; *Rev* 3:20; 19:9). He is the Royal Shepherd, king in docility and in forgiveness, enthroned on the glorious wood of the cross (cf. *Jn* 3:13-15; 12:32; 17:4-5).

That God may be our shepherd

Psalm 23 invites us to renew our trust in God, abandoning ourselves totally in his hands. Let us therefore ask with faith that the Lord also grant us on the difficult ways of our time that we always walk on his paths as a docile and obedient flock, and that he welcome us to his house, to his table, and lead us to "still waters" so that, in accepting the gift of his Spirit, we may quench our thirst at his sources, springs of the living water "welling up to eternal life" (*Jn* 4:14; cf. 7:37-39).

"The Lord has done great things for us"
Psalm 126

In the previous catecheses, we have meditated on a number of psalms of lament and of trust. Today, I would like to reflect with you on a notably joyous Psalm, a prayer that sings with joy the marvels of God. It is Psalm 126 - according to Graeco-Latin numbering, 125 - which extols the great things the Lord has done with his people, and which he continues to do with every believer.

A joyful beginning

The Psalmist begins the prayer in the name of all Israel by recalling the thrilling experience of salvation:

"When the Lord restored the fortunes of Zion,
we were like those who dream.
Then our mouth was filled with laughter,
and our tongue with shouts of joy" (vv. 1-2a).

The Psalm speaks of "restored fortunes": that is, restored to their original state in all their former favourability. It begins then with a situation of suffering and of need to which God responds by bringing about salvation and restoring the man who prays to his former condition, indeed, one that is enriched and even changed for the better. This is what happens to Job, when the Lord restores to him all that he had lost, redoubling it and bestowing upon him an even greater blessing (cf. *Jb* 42:10-13), and this is what the people of Israel experience in returning to their homeland after the Babylonian exile.

Return from exile

This Psalm is meant to be interpreted with reference to the end of the deportation to a foreign land: the expression "restore the fortunes of Zion" is read and understood by the tradition as a "return of the prisoners of Zion". In fact, the return from exile is paradigmatic of every divine and saving intervention, since the fall of Jerusalem and the deportation into Babylon were devastating experiences for the Chosen People, not only on the political and social planes, but also and especially on the religious and spiritual ones. The loss of their land, the end of the Davidic monarchy and the destruction of the Temple appear as a denial of the divine promises, and the people of the Covenant, dispersed among the pagans, painfully question a God who seems to have abandoned them.

Therefore, the end of the deportation and their return to their homeland are experienced as a marvellous return to faith, to trust, to communion with the Lord; it is a "restoring of fortunes" that involves a conversion of heart, forgiveness, re-found friendship with God, knowledge of his mercy and a renewed possibility of praising him (cf.

Jr 29:12-14; 30:18-20; 33:6-11; *Ezk* 39:25-29). It is an experience of overflowing joy, of laughter and of cries of jubilation, so beautiful that "it seems like a dream". Divine help often takes surprising forms that surpass what man is able to imagine; hence the wonder and joy that are expressed in this Psalm: "The Lord has done great things". This is what the nations said, and it is what Israel proclaims:

"Then they said among the nations,
'the Lord has done great things for them.'
The Lord has done great things for us;
we are glad" (vv. 2b-3).

The Lord loves Israel

God performs marvellous works in the history of men. In carrying out salvation, he reveals himself to all as the powerful and merciful Lord, a refuge for the oppressed, who does not forget the cry of the poor (cf. *Ps* 9:10,13), who loves justice and right and of whose love the earth is filled (cf. *Ps* 33:5). Thus, standing before the liberation of the people of Israel, all the nations recognise the great and marvellous things God has accomplished for his people, and they celebrate the Lord in his reality as Saviour. And Israel echoes the proclamation of the nations, taking it up and repeating it once more - but as the protagonist - as a direct recipient of the divine action: "The Lord has done great things for us"; "for us" or even more precisely, "with us", in Hebrew *"immanû"*, thus affirming that privileged relationship that the Lord keeps with his chosen ones, and which is found in the name *Emmanuel*, "God with us", the name by which Jesus would be called, his complete and full revelation (cf. *Mt* 1:23).

Gratitude to God

In our prayer we should look more often at how, in the events of our own lives, the Lord has protected, guided and helped us, and we should praise him for all he has done and does for us. We should be more attentive to the good things the Lord gives to us. We are always attentive to problems and to difficulties, and we are almost unwilling to perceive that there are beautiful things that come from the Lord. This attention, which becomes gratitude, is very important for us; it creates in us a memory for the good and it helps us also in times of darkness. God accomplishes great things, and whoever experiences this - attentive to the Lord's goodness with an attentiveness of heart - is filled with joy. The first part of the Psalm concludes on this joyous note. To be saved and to return to one's homeland from exile are like being returned to life: freedom opens up to laughter, but is does so together with a waiting for a fulfilment still desired and implored.

A full return

The second part of our Psalm continues:

> "Restore our fortunes, O Lord,
> like the watercourses in the Negeb!
> May those who sow in tears reap with shouts of joy!
> He that goes forth weeping,
> bearing the seed for sowing,
> shall come home with shouts of joy,
> bringing his sheaves with him" (vv. 4-6).

If at the beginning of the prayer the Psalmist celebrated the joy of a fortune already restored by the Lord, now instead he asks for it as something still to be realised. If we apply this Psalm to the return from exile, this apparent contradiction could be explained by Israel's historical experience of a difficult and only partial return to their homeland, which prompts the man who prays to implore further divine help to bring the people's restoration to completeness.

But the Psalm goes beyond the purely historical moment and opens to broader, theological dimensions. The consoling experience of freedom from Babylon is nevertheless still incomplete; it has "already" occurred, but it is "not yet" marked by a definitive fullness. Thus, while the prayer joyously celebrates the salvation received, it opens in anticipation of its full realisation. Therefore, the Psalm uses distinctive imagery that in its complexity calls to mind the mysterious reality of redemption, in which the gift received and yet still to be awaited, life and death, joys dreamed of and painful tears, are interwoven.

Imagery of the Psalm

The first image refers to the dried-up streams of the Negeb desert, which with the rains are filled with rushing waters that restore life to the arid ground and make it flourish. Thus, the Psalmist's request is that the restoration of the people's fortunes and their return from exile be like those waters, roaring and unstoppable, capable of transforming the desert into an immense stretch of green grass and flowers.

The second image shifts from the arid and rocky hills of the Negeb to the fields that farmers cultivate for food. In describing salvation, the experience renewed every year in the world of agriculture is here recalled: the difficult and tiring time of sowing, and then the overflowing joy in the harvest. It is a sowing in tears, since one casts to the ground what could still become bread, exposing it to a time of waiting that is full of uncertainty: the farmer works, he prepares the earth, he scatters the seed, but as the parable of the Sower illustrates well, one never knows where the seed will fall - if the birds will eat it, if it will take root, if it will become an ear of grain (cf. *Mt* 13:3-9; *Mk* 4:2-9; *Lk* 8:4-8).

The Lord acts in human history

To scatter the seed is an act of trust and of hope; man's industriousness is needed, but then one must enter into a powerless time of waiting, well aware that many deciding factors will determine the success of the harvest, and that the risk of failure is always lurking. And yet, year after year, the farmer repeats his gesture and scatters the seed. And when it becomes an ear of grain, and the fields fill with crops, this is the joy of he who stands before an extraordinary marvel.

Jesus knew well this experience, and he spoke of it with those who were his own: "He said: 'The kingdom of God is as if a man should scatter seed upon the ground, and should sleep and rise night and day, and the seed should sprout and grow, he knows not how'" (*Mk* 4:26-27). It is the hidden mystery of life, these are the wondrous, "great things" of salvation that the Lord carries out in human history and whose secret men do not know.

From darkness to light

When divine help is manifested in all its fullness, it has an overflowing dimension, like the watercourses of the Negeb and like the grain of the fields - the latter also evoking a disproportion that is characteristic of the things of God: a disproportion between the effort of the sowing and the immense joy of the harvest; between the anxiety of waiting and the comforting vision of the granaries filled; between the little seeds thrown upon the ground and the great sheaves of grain made golden by the sun. At the harvest, all is transformed; the weeping has ended and has given way to an exultant cry of joy.

This is what the Psalmist refers to when he speaks of salvation, of liberation, of the restoration of fortunes and of return from exile. The deportation to Babylon, like every other situation of suffering and of crisis, with its painful darkness filled with doubts and the apparent absence of God, in reality - our Psalm says - is like a time of sowing. In the Mystery of Christ - in the light of the New Testament - the message becomes even clearer and more explicit: the believer who passes through this darkness is like the grain of wheat that falls into the earth and dies, but that bears much fruit (cf. *Jn* 12:24); or, borrowing another image that was dear to Jesus, the believer is like the woman who suffers the pains of labour for the sake of attaining the joy of having brought a new life to light (cf. *Jn* 16:21).

God is always present

This Psalm teaches us that, in our prayer, we must always remain open to hope, and firm in our faith in God. Our personal history - even if often marked by suffering, uncertainty and moments of crisis - is a history of salvation and of the "restoring of fortunes". In Jesus our every exile ends and every tear is wiped away in the mystery of his cross, of death transformed into life, like the grain of wheat that falls into the earth and yields a harvest. Also for us, this discovery of Jesus Christ is the great joy of God's "yes", of the restoration of our fortunes. But like those who - having returned from Babylon filled with joy - found an impoverished, devastated land as well as difficulty in sowing, and who, weeping, suffered not knowing if at the end there would actually be a harvest, so also we, after the great discovery of Jesus Christ - our life, the truth, the way - entering into the terrain of faith, into the "land of faith", we also often find that life is dark, hard, difficult - a sowing in tears - but we are certain that in the end, the light of Christ truly gives us the great harvest.

And we must learn this also in the dark nights; do not forget that the light is there, that God is already in the midst of our lives and that we can sow with the great trust in the fact that God's "yes" is stronger than us all. It is important not to lose the memory of God's presence in our lives, this profound joy that God has entered into our lives, thus freeing us: it is gratitude for the discovery of Jesus Christ, who has come among us. And this gratitude is transformed into hope; it is a star of hope that gives us trust; it is light, since the very pains of sowing are the beginning of new life, of the great and definitive joy of God.

The Great Hallel: Psalm 136 (135)

Today I would like to meditate with you on a Psalm that sums up the entire history of salvation recorded in the Old Testament. It is a great hymn of praise that celebrates the Lord in the multiple, repeated expressions of his goodness throughout human history: it is Psalm 136, or 135 according to the Graeco-Latin tradition.

Manifestation of God's love

A solemn prayer of thanksgiving, known as the "Great Hallel", this Psalm is traditionally sung at the end of the Jewish Passover meal and was probably also prayed by Jesus at the Last Supper celebrated with his disciples. In fact, the annotation of the Evangelists, "and when they had sung a hymn, they went out to the Mount of Olives" (cf. *Mt* 26:30; *Mk* 14:26), would seem to allude to it. The horizon of praise thus appears to illumine the difficult path to Golgotha. The whole of Psalm 136 unfolds in the form of a litany, marked by the antiphonal refrain: "For his steadfast love endures for ever". The many wonders God has worked in human history and his continuous intervention on behalf of his people are listed in the composition. Furthermore, to every proclamation of the Lord's saving action the antiphon responds with the basic impetus of praise. The eternal love of God is a love which, in accordance with the Hebrew term used, suggestive of fidelity, mercy, kindness, grace and tenderness, is the unifying motif of the entire Psalm. The refrain always takes the same form, whereas the regular paradigmatic manifestations of God's love change: Creation, liberation through the Exodus, the gift of land, the Lord's provident and constant help for his people and for every created being.

God the creator

After a triple invitation to give thanks to God as sovereign (vv. 1-3), the Lord is celebrated as the One who works "great wonders" (v. 4), the first of which is the Creation: the heavens, the earth, the heavenly bodies (vv. 5-9). The created world is not merely a scenario into which God's saving action is inserted, but rather is the very beginning of that marvellous action. With the Creation, the Lord shows himself in all his goodness and beauty, he commits himself to life, revealing a desire for goodness which gives rise to every other action of salvation. And in our Psalm, re-echoing the first chapter of Genesis, the principal elements of the created world are summed up, with special insistence on the heavenly bodies, the sun, the moon and the stars, magnificent created things that govern the day and the night. Nothing is said here of the creation of human beings but they are ever present; the sun and the moon are for them - for men and women - so as to structure human time, setting it in relation to the Creator, especially by denoting the liturgical seasons.

God the liberator

And it is precisely the Feast of Easter that is immediately evoked, when, passing to God's manifestation of himself in history, the great event of the Exodus, freedom from slavery in Egypt, begins, whose most significant elements are outlined: the liberation from Egypt, beginning with the plague of killing the Egyptian firstborn, the Exodus from Egypt, the crossing of the Red Sea, the journey through the desert, the entry into the Promised Land (vv. 10-20). This is the very first moment of Israel's history; God intervened powerfully to lead his people to freedom; through Moses, his envoy, he asserted himself before Pharaoh, revealing himself in his full grandeur, and at last broke down the resistance of the Egyptians with the terrible plague of the death of the firstborn. Israel could thus leave the country of slavery taking with it the gold of its oppressors (cf. *Ex* 12:35-36), "defiantly" (*Ex* 14:8), in the exulting sign of victory.

God the protector

At the Red Sea, too, the Lord acted with merciful power. Before an Israel so terrified by the sight of the Egyptians in pursuit as to regret its departure from Egypt (cf. *Ex*

14:10-12), God, as our Psalm says, "divided the Red Sea in sunder... and made the people of Israel pass through the midst of it... but overthrew Pharaoh and his host" (136:13-15). The image of the Red Sea "divided" into two seems to call to mind the idea of the sea as a great monster hacked into two and thereby rendered harmless. The might of the Lord overcomes the danger of the forces of nature and of these soldiers deployed in battle array by men: the sea, which seemed to bar the way of the People of God, let Israel cross on dry ground and then swept over the Egyptians, submerging them. Thus the full salvific force of the Lord's "mighty hand, and an outstretched arm" (cf. *Dt* 5:15; 7:19; 26:8) was demonstrated: the unjust oppressor was vanquished, engulfed by the waters, while the People of God "walked on dry ground through the sea", continuing its journey to freedom.

God in the desert

Our Psalm now refers to this journey, recalling in one short phrase Israel's long pilgrimage toward the promised land: he "led his people through the wilderness, for his steadfast love endures for ever" (v. 16). These few words refer to a 40-year experience, a crucial period for Israel, which, in letting itself be guided by the Lord, learned to live in faith, obedience and docility to God's law. These were difficult years, marked by hardship in the desert, but also happy years, trusting in the Lord with filial trust. It was

the time of "youth", as the Prophet Jeremiah describes it
in speaking to Israel in the Lord's name with words full
of tenderness and nostalgia: "I remember the devotion of
your youth, your love as a bride, how you followed me
in the wilderness, in a land not sown" (*Jr* 2:2). The Lord,
like the shepherd of Psalm 23[22] whom we contemplated
in a Catechesis, for 40 years guided, taught and cherished
his people, leading it right to the promised land, also
overcoming the resistance and hostility of enemy peoples
that wished to block its way to salvation (cf. 136:17-20).

God gives

So as the "great wonders" that our Psalm lists unfold, we
reach the moment of the conclusive gift, the fulfilment of
the divine promise made to the Fathers: "Gave their land
as a heritage, for his steadfast love endures for ever; a
heritage to Israel his servant, for his steadfast love endures
for ever" (136:21-22). Then, in celebrating the Lord's
eternal love, the gift of land was commemorated, a gift
that the people were to receive but without ever taking
possession of it, continuing to live in an attitude of grateful
acknowledgement and gratitude. Israel received the land
it was to live in as "a heritage", a generic term which
designates the possession of a good received from another
person, a right of ownership which specifically refers to the
paternal patrimony. One of God's prerogatives is "giving";
and now, at the end of the journey of the Exodus, Israel,

the recipient of the gift, enters as a son or daughter the land of the promise now fulfilled. The time of wandering, of living in tents, of living a precarious life, is over. It was then that the happy period of permanence began, of joy in building houses, of planting vineyards, of living in security (cf. *Dt* 8:7-13). Yet it was also the time of the temptation to idolatry, contamination with pagans, self-sufficiency that led to the Origin of the gift being forgotten. Accordingly, the Psalmist mentions Israel's humiliation and the foe, a mortal reality in which the Lord once again reveals himself as Saviour: "He...remembered us in our low estate, for his steadfast love endures for ever; and rescued us from our foes, for his steadfast love endures for ever" (136:23-24).

Israel remembers God's love

At this point a question arises: how can we make this Psalm our own prayer, how can we ourselves claim this Psalm as our own prayer? What is important is the Psalm's setting, for at the beginning and at the end is the Creation. Let us return to this point: the Creation as God's great gift by which we live and in which he reveals himself in his great goodness. Therefore, to think of the Creation as a gift of God is a common point for all of us. The history of salvation then follows. We can of course say: this liberation from Egypt, the time in the desert, the entry into the Holy Land and all the other subsequent problems are very remote from us, they are not part of our own history.

Yet we must be attentive to the fundamental structure of this prayer. The basic structure is that Israel remembers the Lord's goodness. In this history, dark valleys, arduous journeys and death succeed one another but Israel recalls that God was good and that it can survive in this dark valley, in this valley of death, because it remembers. It remembers the Lord's goodness and his power; his mercy is effective for ever. And this is also important for us: to remember the Lord's goodness. Memory strongly sustains hope. Memory tells us: God exists, God is good, his mercy endures for ever. So it is that memory unfolds, even in the darkest day or time, showing the way towards the future. It represents "great lights" and is our guiding star. We too have good memories of the goodness, of God's merciful love that endures for ever.

God's mercy is eternal

Israel's history is a former memory for us, too, of how God revealed himself, how he created a people of his own. Then God became man, one of us: he lived with us, he suffered with us, he died for us. He stays with us in the Sacrament and in the Word. It is a history, a memory of God's goodness that assures us of his goodness: his love endures for ever. And then, in these 2,000 years of the Church's history there is always, again and again, the Lord's goodness. After the dark period of the Nazi and Communist persecution, God set us free, he showed that he is good, that he is powerful, that his mercy endures for ever. And, as in our common, collective history, this memory of God's goodness is present, it helps us and becomes for us a star of hope so that each one also has his or her personal story of salvation. We must truly treasure this story, and in order to trust must keep ever present in our mind the memory of the great things he has also worked in my life: his mercy endures for ever. And if today I am immersed in the dark night, tomorrow he sets me free, for his mercy is eternal.

Our daily bread

Let us return to the Psalm, because at the end it returns to the Creation. The Lord, it says, "gives food to all flesh, for his steadfast love endures for ever" (v. 25). The prayer of the Psalm concludes with an invitation to praise: "Give thanks to the God of heaven, for his steadfast love endures for ever". The Lord is our good and provident Father, who gives his children their heritage and lavishes life-giving food upon all. God who created the heavens and the earth and the great heavenly bodies, who entered human history to bring all his children to salvation is the God who fills the universe with his presence of goodness, caring for life and providing bread. The invisible power of the Creator and Lord of which the Psalm sings is revealed in the humble sign of the bread he gives us, with which he enables us to live. And so it is that this daily bread symbolises and sums up the love of God as Father and opens us to the fulfilment of the New Testament, to that "Bread of Life", the Eucharist, which accompanies us in our lives as believers, anticipating the definitive joy of the messianic banquet in heaven.

God's love for us

The praise and blessing of Psalm 136[135] has made us review the most important stages in the history of salvation, to reach the Paschal Mystery in which God's saving action reaches its culmination. Let us therefore celebrate with grateful joy the Creator, Saviour and faithful Father, who "so loved the world that he gave his only Son, that whoever believes in him should not perish but have eternal life" (*Jn* 3:16). In the fullness of time, the Son of God became man to give life, for the salvation of each one of us, and gave himself as bread in the Eucharistic mystery to enable us to enter his Covenant which makes us his children. May both God's merciful goodness and his sublime "steadfast love for ever" reach far afield.

I would therefore like to conclude this Catechesis by making my own the words that St John wrote in his First Letter and that we must always have in mind in our prayers: "See what love the Father has given us, that we should be called children of God; and so we are" (*1 Jn* 3:1).

The Great Song of the "Law": Psalm 119 (118)

In previous Catecheses we have meditated on several Psalms that are examples of typical forms of prayer: lamentation, trust and praise. In today's Catechesis I would like to reflect on Psalm 119, according to the Hebrew tradition, Psalm 118 according to the Graeco-Latin one. It is a very special Psalm, unique of its kind. This is first of all because of its length. Indeed, it is composed of 176 verses divided into 22 stanzas of eight verses each. Moreover, its special feature is that it is an "acrostic in alphabetical order", in other words it is structured in accordance with the Hebrew alphabet, which consists of 22 letters. Each stanza begins with a letter of this alphabet and the first letter of the first word of each of the eight verses in the stanza begins with this letter. This is both original and indeed a demanding literary genre in which the author of the Psalm must have had to summon up all his skill.

The Law of God

However, what is most important for us is this Psalm's central theme. In fact, it is an impressive, solemn canticle on the *Torah* of the Lord, that is, on his Law, a term which in its broadest and most comprehensive meaning should be understood as a teaching, an instruction, a rule of life. The *Torah* is a revelation, it is a word of God that challenges the human being and elicits his response of trusting obedience and generous love. This Psalm is steeped in love for the word of God whose beauty, saving power and capacity for giving joy and life it celebrates; because the divine Law is not the heavy yoke of slavery but a liberating gift of grace that brings happiness. "I will delight in your statutes; I will not forget your word", the Psalmist declares (v. 16), and then: "Lead me in the path of your commandments, for I delight in it" (v. 35). And further: "Oh, how I love your law! It is my meditation all the day" (v. 97). The Law of the Lord, his word, is the centre of the praying person's life; he finds comfort in it, he makes it the subject of meditation, he treasures it in his heart: "I have laid up your word in my heart, that I might not sin against you" (v. 11), and this is the secret of the Psalmist's happiness; and then, again, "the godless besmear me with lies, but with my whole heart I keep your precepts" (v. 69).

The Blessed Virgin

The Psalmist's faithfulness stems from listening to the word, from pondering on it in his inmost self, meditating on it and cherishing it, just as did Mary, who "kept all these things, pondering them in her heart" - the words that had been addressed to her and the marvellous events in which

God revealed himself, asking her for the assent of her faith (cf. *Lk* 2:19,51). And if the first verses of our Psalm begin by proclaiming "blessed" those "who walk in the law of the Lord" (v. 1b), and "who keep his testimonies" (v. 2a), then it is once again the Virgin Mary who brings to completion the perfect figure of the believer, described by the Psalmist. It is she, in fact, who is the true "blessed", proclaimed such by Elizabeth because "she... believed that there would be a fulfilment of what was spoken to her from the Lord" (*Lk* 1:45). Moreover it was to her and to her faith that Jesus himself bore witness when he answered the woman who had cried: "Blessed is the womb that bore you", with "Blessed rather are those who hear the word of God and keep it!" (*Lk* 11:27-28). Of course, Mary is blessed because she carried the Saviour in her womb, but especially because she accepted God's announcement and because she was an attentive and loving custodian of his word.

Constant trust in God

Psalm 119 is thus woven around this word of life and blessedness. If its central theme is the "word" and "Law" of the Lord, next to these terms in almost all the verses such synonyms recur as "precepts", "statutes", "commandments", "ordinances", "promises", "judgement"; and then so many verbs relating to them such as observe, keep, understand, learn, love, meditate and live. The entire alphabet unfolds through the 22 stanzas of this Psalm and also the whole of the vocabulary of the believer's trusting relationship with God; we find in it praise, thanksgiving and trust, but also supplication and lamentation. However, they are always imbued with the certainty of divine grace and of the power of the word of God. Even the verses more heavily marked by grief and by a sense of darkness remain open to hope and are permeated by faith. "My soul cleaves to the dust; revive me according to your word" (v. 25), the Psalmist trustingly prays. "I have become like a wineskin in the smoke, yet I have not forgotten your statutes" (v. 83), is his cry as a believer. His fidelity, even when it is put to the test, finds strength in the Lord's word: "then shall I have an answer for those who taunt me, for I trust in your word" (v. 42), he says firmly; and even when he faces the anguishing prospect of death, the Lord's commandments are his reference point and his hope of victory: "they have almost made an end of me on earth; but I have not forsaken your precepts" (v. 87).

Follow Christ to follow the Law

The Law of the Lord, the object of the passionate love of the Psalmist as well as of every believer, is a source of life. The desire to understand it, to observe it and to direct the whole of one's being by it is the characteristic of every righteous person who is faithful to the Lord, and who "on his law... meditates day and night", as Psalm 1 recites (v. 2). The law of God must be kept "upon the heart", as the well known text of the *Shema* in Deuteronomy says: "Hear, O Israel: And these words which I command you this day shall be upon your heart; and you shall teach them diligently to your children, and shall talk of them when you sit in your house, and when you walk by the way, and when you lie down, and when you rise" (6:4,6-7).

The Law of God, at the centre of life, demands that the heart listen. It is a listening that does not consist of servile, but rather of filial, trusting and aware obedience. Listening to the word is a personal encounter with the Lord of life, an encounter that must be expressed in concrete decisions and become a journey and a "sequela". When Jesus is asked what one should do to inherit eternal life, he points to the way of observance of the Law but indicates what should be done to bring it to completion: "But you lack one thing; go, sell what you have, and give to the poor, and you will have treasure in heaven; and come, follow me!" (*Mk* 10:21ff.). Fulfilment of the Law is the following of Jesus, travelling on the road that Jesus took, in the company of Jesus.

The Lord is my portion

Psalm 119 thus brings us to the encounter with the Lord and orients us to the Gospel. There is a verse in it on which I would now like to reflect: it is verse 57: "the Lord is my portion; I promise to keep his words". In other Psalms too the person praying affirms that the Lord is his "portion", his inheritance: "The Lord is my chosen portion and my cup", Psalm 16[15] says. "God is the strength of my heart and my portion for ever" is the protestation of faith of the faithful person in Psalm 73 [72]: v. 26b, and again, in Psalm 142[141], the Psalmist cries to the Lord: "You are my refuge, my portion in the land of the living" (v. 5b).

The tribe of Levi

This term "portion" calls to mind the event of the division of the promised land between the tribes of Israel, when no piece of land was assigned to the Levites because their "portion" was the Lord himself. Two texts of the Pentateuch, using the term in question, are explicit in this regard: "Then the Lord said to Aaron: 'You shall have no inheritance in their land, neither shall you have any *portion* among them; I am your *portion* and your inheritance among the people of Israel'", as the Book of Numbers (18:20) declares and as Deuteronomy reaffirms: "Therefore Levi has no *portion* or inheritance with his brothers; the Lord is his inheritance, as the Lord your God said to him" (*Dt* 10:9; cf. *Dt* 18:2; *Jos* 13:33; E*zk* 44:28).

The Priests, who belong to the tribe of Levi, cannot be landowners in the land that God was to bequeath as a legacy to his people, thus bringing to completion the promise he had made to Abraham (cf. *Gn* 12:1-7). The ownership of land, a fundamental element for permanence and for survival, was a sign of blessing because it presupposed the possibility of building a house, of raising children, of cultivating the fields and of living on the produce of the earth. Well, the Levites, mediators of the sacred and of the divine blessing, unlike the other Israelites could not own possessions, this external sign of blessing and source of subsistence. Totally dedicated to the Lord, they had to live on him alone, reliant on his provident love and on the generosity of their brethren without any other inheritance since God was their portion, God was the land that enabled them to live to the full.

The word of God

The person praying in Psalm 119 then applies this reality to himself: "The Lord is my portion". His love for God and for his word leads him to make the radical decision to have the Lord as his one possession and also to treasure his words as a precious gift more valuable than any legacy or earthly possession. There are two different ways in which our verse may be translated and it could also be translated as "My portion Lord, as I have said, is to preserve your words". The two translations are not contradictory but on the contrary complete each other: the Psalmist meant that his portion was the Lord but that preserving the divine words was also part of his inheritance, as he was to say later in v. 111: "Your testimonies are my heritage for ever; yea, they are the joy of my heart". This is the happiness of the Psalmist: like the Levites, he has been given the word of God as his portion, his inheritance.

Our portion of the Promised Land

These verses are also of great importance for all of us. First of all for priests, who are called to live on the Lord and his word alone with no other means of security, with him as their one possession and as their only source of true life. In this light one understands the free choice of celibacy for the Kingdom of Heaven in order to rediscover it in its beauty and power. Yet these verses are also important for all the faithful, the People of God that belong to him alone, "a kingdom of priests" for the Lord (cf. *1 P* 2:9; *Rv* 1:6,5:10), called to the radicalism of the Gospel, witnesses of the life brought by Christ, the new and definitive "High Priest" who gave himself as a sacrifice for the salvation of the world (cf. *Heb* 2:17; 4:14-16; 5:5-10; 9,11ff.). The Lord and his word: these are our "land", in which to live in communion and in joy.

A way to happiness

Let us therefore permit the Lord to instil this love for his word in our hearts and to grant that we may always place him and his holy will at the centre of our life. Let us ask that our prayers and the whole of our life be illuminated by the word of God, the lamp to light our footsteps and a light on our path, as Psalm 119 (cf. v. 105) says, so that we may walk safely in the land of men. And may Mary, who generously welcomed the Word, be our guide and comfort, the polestar that indicates the way to happiness.

Then we too shall be able to rejoice in our prayers, like the praying person of Psalm 16, in the unexpected gifts of the Lord and in the undeserved legacy that fell to us: "The Lord is my chosen portion and my cup... the lines have fallen for me in pleasant places; yea, I have a goodly heritage" (*Ps* 16:5,6).

Christ the King: Psalm 110 (109)

Today I would like to end my catechesis on the prayer of the Book of Psalms by meditating on one of the most famous of the "royal Psalms", a Psalm that Jesus himself cited and that the New Testament authors referred to extensively and interpreted as referring to the Messiah, to Christ. It is Psalm 110 according to the Hebrew tradition, 109 according to the Graeco-Latin one, a Psalm very dear to the ancient Church and to believers of all times. This prayer may at first have been linked to the enthronement of a Davidic king; yet its meaning exceeds the specific contingency of an historic event, opening to broader dimensions and thereby becoming a celebration of the victorious Messiah, glorified at God's right hand.

God enthrones the king

The Psalm begins with a solemn declaration:

"The Lord says to my lord 'Sit at my right hand, till I make your enemies your footstool'" (v. 1).

God himself enthrones the king in glory, seating him at his right, a sign of very great honour and of absolute privilege. The king is thus admitted to sharing in the divine kingship, of which he is mediator to the people. The king's kingship is also brought into being in the victory over his adversaries whom God himself places at his feet. The victory over his enemies is the Lord's, but the king is enabled to share in it and his triumph becomes a sign and testimony of divine power.

In the New Testament

The royal glorification expressed at the beginning of the Psalm was adopted by the New Testament as a messianic prophecy. For this reason the verse is among those most frequently used by New Testament authors, either as an explicit quotation or as an allusion. With regard to the Messiah, Jesus himself mentioned this verse in order to show that the Messiah was greater than David, that he was David's Lord (cf. *Mt* 22:41-45; *Mk* 12:35-37; *Lk* 20:41-44). And Peter returned to it in his discourse at Pentecost, proclaiming that this enthronement of the king was brought about in the resurrection of Christ and that Christ was henceforth seated at the right hand of the Father, sharing in God's kingship over the world (cf. *Ac* 2:29-35).

Christ is this King

Indeed, Christ is the enthroned Lord, the Son of Man seated at the right hand of God and coming on the clouds of heaven, as Jesus described himself during the trial before the Sanhedrin (cf. *Mt* 26:63-64; *Mk* 14:61-62; cf. also *Lk* 22:66-69). He is the true King who, with the Resurrection,

entered into glory at the right hand of the Father (*Rm* 8:34;
Ep 2:5; *Col* 3:1; *Heb* 8:1; 12:2), was made superior to
angels, and seated in heaven above every power with every
adversary at his feet, until the time when the last enemy,
death, was to be defeated by him once and for all (cf. *1
Co* 15:24-26; *Ep* 1:20-23; *Hb* 1:3-4; 2:5-8; 10:12-13; *1
P* 3:22). And we immediately understand that this king,
seated at the right hand of God, who shares in his kingship,
is not one of those who succeeded David, but is actually
the new David, the Son of God who triumphed over death
and truly shares in God's glory. He is our king, who also
gives us eternal life.

Office from the Lord

Hence an indissoluble relationship exists between the king
celebrated by our Psalm and God. The two of them govern
together as one, so that the Psalmist can say that it is God
himself who extends the sovereign's sceptre, giving him
the task of ruling over his adversaries as verse 2 says: "The
Lord sends forth from Zion your mighty sceptre. Rule in
the midst of your foes!"

The exercise of power is an office that the king receives
directly from the Lord, a responsibility which he must
exercise in dependence and obedience, thereby becoming
a sign, within the people, of God's powerful and provident
presence. Dominion over his foes, glory and victory are
gifts received that make the sovereign a mediator of the

Lord's triumph over evil. He subjugates his enemies, transforming them; he wins them over with his love.

Divine procreation

For this reason the king's greatness is celebrated in the following verse. In fact the interpretation of verse 3 presents some difficulty. In the original Hebrew text a reference was made to the mustering of the army to which the people generously responded, gathering round their sovereign on the day of his coronation. The Greek translation of The Septuagint that dates back to between the second and third centuries BC refers, however, to the divine sonship of the king, to his birth or begetting on the part of the Lord. This is the interpretation that has been chosen by the Church, which is why the verse reads like this: "Yours is princely power in the day of your birth, in holy splendour; before the daystar, like the dew, I have begotten you".

This divine oracle concerning the king would thus assert a divine procreation, steeped in splendour and mystery, a secret and inscrutable origin linked to the arcane beauty of dawn and to the miracle of dew that sparkles in the fields in the early morning light and makes them fertile. In this way, the figure of the king, indissolubly bound to the heavenly reality, who really comes from God, is outlined, the Messiah who brings divine life to the people and is the mediator of holiness and salvation. Here too we see that all this is not achieved by the figure of a Davidic king but by the Lord Jesus Christ, who really comes from God; he is the light that brings divine life to the world.

King and priest

The first stanza of the Psalm ends with this evocative and enigmatic image. It is followed by another oracle, which unfolds a new perspective along the lines of a priestly dimension connected with kingship. Verse 4 says: "The Lord has sworn and will not change his mind, 'You are a priest for ever after the order of Melchizedek'".

Melchizedek was the priest-king of Salem who had blessed Abraham and offered him bread and wine after the victorious military campaign the patriarch led to rescue his nephew Lot from the hands of enemies who had captured him (cf. *Gn* 14). Royal and priestly power converge in the figure of Melchizedek. They are then proclaimed by the Lord in a declaration that promises eternity: the king celebrated in the Psalm will be a priest for ever, the mediator of the Lord's presence among his people, the intermediary of the blessing that comes from God, who, in liturgical action, responds to it with the human answer of blessing.

The Letter to the Hebrews makes an explicit reference to this verse (cf. 5:5-6,10; 6:19-20) focusing on it the whole of chapter seven and developing its reflection on Christ's priesthood. Jesus, as the Letter to the Hebrews tells us in the light of Psalm 110[109], is the true and definitive priest who brings to fulfilment and perfects the features of Melchizedek's priesthood.

Christ fulfils the prophecy of Melchizedek

Melchizedek, as the Letter to the Hebrews says, was "without father or mother or genealogy" (7:3a), hence not a priest according to the dynastic rules of Levitical priesthood. Consequently he "continues a priest for ever" (7:3c), a prefiguration of Christ, the perfect High Priest who "has become a priest, not according to a legal requirement concerning bodily descent but by the power of an indestructible life" (7:16). In the Risen Lord Jesus who had ascended into heaven where he is seated at the right hand of the Father the prophecy of our Psalm is fulfilled and the priesthood of Melchizedek is brought to completion. This is because, rendered absolute and eternal, it became a reality that never fades (cf. 7:24). And the offering of bread and wine made by Melchizedek in Abraham's time is fulfilled in the Eucharistic action of Jesus who offers himself in the bread and in the wine and, having conquered death, brings life to all believers. Since he is an eternal priest, "holy, blameless, unstained" (7:26), as the Letter to the Hebrews states further, "he is able for all time to save those who draw near to God through him, since he always lives to make intercession for them" (7:25).

The Lord protects the king

After this divine pronouncement in verse 4, with its solemn oath, the scene of the Psalm changes and the poet, addressing the king directly, proclaims: "The Lord is at your right hand" (*Ps* 110:5a). If in verse 1 it was the king who was seated at God's right hand as a sign of supreme prestige and honour, the Lord now takes his place at the right of the sovereign to protect him with this shield in battle and save him from every peril. The king was safe, God is his champion and they fight together and defeat every evil.

Thus the last verses of the Psalm open with the vision of the triumphant sovereign. Supported by the Lord, having received both power and glory from him (cf. v. 2), he opposes his foes, crushing his adversaries and judging the nations. The scene is painted in strong colours to signify the drama of the battle and the totality of the royal victory. The sovereign, protected by the Lord, demolishes every obstacle and moves ahead safely to victory. He tells us: yes, there is widespread evil in the world, there is an ongoing battle between good and evil and it seems as though evil were the stronger. No, the Lord is stronger, Christ, our true King and Priest, for he fights with all God's power, and in spite of all the things that make us doubt the positive outcome of history, Christ wins and good wins, love wins rather than hatred.

Enigmatic ending

The evocative image that concludes our Psalm fits in here; it is also an enigmatic verse: "He will drink from the brook by the way; therefore he will lift up his head" (v. 7).

The king's figure stands out in the middle of the description of the battle. At a moment of respite and rest he quenches his thirst at a stream, finding in it refreshment and fresh strength to continue on his triumphant way, holding his head high as a sign of definitive victory. It is clear that these deeply enigmatic words were a challenge for the Fathers of the Church because of the different interpretations they could be given. Thus, for example, St Augustine said: "This brook is the onward flow of the human being, of humanity, and Christ did not disdain to drink of this brook, becoming man; and so it was that on entering the humanity of the human being he lifted up his head and is now the Head of the mystical Body, he is our head, he is the definitive winner" (cf. *Enarrationes in Psalmos* CIX, 20: PL36, 1462).

The Psalm is fulfilled in Christ

Following the lines of the New Testament translation, the Church's Tradition has held this Psalm in high esteem as one of the most important messianic texts. And the Fathers continued eminently to refer to it in a Christological key. The king of whom the Psalmist sang is ultimately Christ, the Messiah who establishes the Kingdom of God and overcomes the powers of evil. He is the Word, begotten by the Father before every creature, before the dawn, the Son incarnate who died and rose and is seated in heaven, the eternal priest who through the mystery of the bread and wine bestows forgiveness of sins and gives reconciliation with God, the king who lifts up his head, triumphing over death with his resurrection. It would suffice to remember a passage, once again in St Augustine's commentary on this Psalm, where he writes: "It was necessary to know the Only-Begotten Son of God who was about to come among men, to adopt man and to become a man by taking on his nature; he died, rose and ascended into Heaven, he is seated at the right hand of the Father and fulfilled among the people all that he had promised.... All this, therefore, had to be prophesied, it had to be foretold, to be pointed out as destined to come about, so that by coming unexpectedly it would not give rise to fear but by having been foretold, would then be accepted with faith, joy and expectation. This Psalm fits into the context of these promises. It prophesies our Lord and Saviour Jesus Christ in such reliable and explicit terms that we cannot have the slightest doubt that it is really Christ who is proclaimed in it" (cf. *Enarrationes in Psalmos* CIX, 3: PL 36,1447).

May we follow Christ

The paschal event of Christ thus becomes the reality to which the Psalm invites us to look, to look at Christ to understand the meaning of true kingship, to live in service and in the gift of self, in a journey of obedience and love "to the end" (cf. *Jn* 13:1 and 19:30). In praying with this Psalm let us therefore ask the Lord to enable us to proceed on his paths, in the following of Christ, the Messiah King, ready to climb with him the mount of the cross to attain glory with him, and to contemplate him seated at the right hand of the Father, a victorious king and a merciful priest who gives forgiveness and salvation to all men and women. And we too, by the grace of God made "a chosen race, a royal priesthood, a holy nation" (cf. *1 P* 2:9), will be able to draw joyfully from the wells of salvation (cf. *Is* 12:3) and proclaim to the whole world the marvels of the One who "called you out of darkness into his marvellous light" (cf. *1 P* 2:9).

Pray with the Psalms

In these recent catecheses I wanted to present to you certain Psalms, precious prayers that we find in the Bible and that reflect the various situations of life and the various states of mind that we may have with regard to God. I would therefore like to renew to you all the invitation to pray with the Psalms, even becoming accustomed to using the Liturgy of the Hours of the Church, Lauds in the morning, Vespers in the evening, and Compline before retiring. Our relationship with God cannot but be enriched with greater joy and trust in the daily journey towards him.

Sources

"Arise, O Lord! Deliver me!" *Psalm 3*: General Audience, 7 September 2011, St Peter's Square.

"My God, my God, why have you forsaken me?" *Psalm 22 (21)*: General Audience, 14 September 2011, Paul VI Audience Hall.

"The Lord is my shepherd: I shall not want" *Psalm 23*: General Audience, 5 October 2011, St Peter's Square.

"The Lord has done great things for us" *Psalm 126*: General Audience, 12 October 2011, St Peter's Square.

The Great Hallel: Psalm 136 (135): General Audience, 19 October 2011, St Peter's Square.

The Great Song of the "Law": Psalm 119 (118): General Audience, 9 November 2011, St Peter's Square.

Christ the King: Psalm 110 (109): General Audience, 16 November 2011, St Peter's Square.